One Red Thread

Discovering the Purpose Already Woven Into Your Life

Dov Baron

Copyright © 2018 Dov Baron

All rights reserved.

Dov Baron

CONTENTS

	Introduction	1
1	Why Discovering Your Personal (and Corporate) Purpose Is Important	3
2	"I'll Be Happy When…"	7
3	Redefining Leaders	9
4	Chapter Four: Passion and Purpose	13
5	Chapter 5: Where Purpose Hides and How to Find It	17
6	Full Monty Purpose Elicitation® Process	19
7	What's Next?	25
	Gratitudes	29
	About the author	33

INTRODUCTION

Picture yourself standing in an art gallery. As you look around at the multiple works of art, a magnificent, beautiful, handmade, multi-colored rug on the wall catches your eye. From where you are standing, the rug seems to have every color of the rainbow woven into it. You are intrigued because somehow this rug has both great complexity and great simplicity in its design.
Walking over to take a closer look, you stand in awe of the beauty and artistry of the piece. Suddenly you notice a small sign on the wall underneath the display.
The sign gives the name of this woven artwork and a brief explanation.
The piece is entitled: "One Red Thread." The description of the piece goes on to say that this rug represents each of our lives. It is the unique combination of the colored threads that together create the tapestry of our lives. The description goes on to say that a single Red Thread is intricately woven throughout the rug. This thread may not be apparent, but it is the very essence of what binds the entire piece together. The description challenges you to look for the One Red Thread in your own tapestry.

CHAPTER 1:

WHY DISCOVERING YOUR PERSONAL (AND CORPORATE) PURPOSE IS IMPORTANT

We all have days where it's hard to get out of bed. For many people, the demands of work and life in general can seem overwhelming on a daily basis. According to The Engaged Workplace, Gallup conducted studies over three years (2017) and learned that fewer than 30 percent of people in the workforce are fully engaged. Forget about springing out of bed, it's hard to even crawl out of the covers to go do something that has little meaning beyond providing the means to pay the rent. Yet miraculously, some folks, no matter what is going on, find a way to not only get out of bed but indeed do spring out of bed.

Look, I get it. It's easy to look at such a person and think they're a different breed of human beings or some kind of freak, but are they? Or, are they pulled out of bed by something bigger than their own discomfort?

I put it to you that those who are doing extraordinary things in their lives and in their businesses are those who are Purpose-driven. But I'm getting ahead of myself. Let's take a look at why you should care.

The Pursuit of Purpose

The pursuit of Purpose, alongside the pursuit of profit, mobilizes people in a way that pursuing profits alone never will. An organization or a person without Purpose manages people and resources while an organization with Purpose inspires, engages, and catalyzes its people and resources.

Purpose is the key ingredient of an authentic leader who inspires loyalty. Purpose is also the highest value asset of a sustainable organizational culture. Purpose, when realized, is woven into the fabric of an extraordinary leader and it becomes the unseen, yet ever-present engine that drives an organization. For a new, emerging company and/or companies who recognize the need for a fresh start, Purpose can be a strategic starting point and an organic attractor of both top talent and customers. In what can appear to be a hyper-competitive environment, there is no greater differentiator than Purpose. For an individual and or a company to thrive in today's global marketplace, we need to infuse Purpose in all that we do.

The Case for Purpose

Look, if you think Purpose is "soft skills" or somehow "fluffy" leadership think again! In 2010, IMD's Center for Corporate Sustainability research validated the importance corporate Purpose plays in employee and client retention and in impacting financial performance. Loyalty isn't built on just money. Employees who are working towards a cause increased their productivity by up to 30 percent.

In a survey titled "The Business Case for Purpose," a team from Harvard Business Review Analytics and professional services firm EY's Beacon institute declares: *"a new leading edge: those companies able to harness the power of purpose to drive performance and profitability enjoy a distinct competitive advantage."* Ninety percent of respondents in the study said their company understood the importance of purpose, but less than half thought it ran in a purpose-driven way. In every organization, whether its people realize it or not, *"there is a systemic relationship between purpose (what we are here to do), measures (how we know how we are doing) and method (how we do it)."*[1]

In their book ***Corporate Culture and Performance***, authors John Kotter and James Heskett show that over a decade-long period, purposeful, value-driven companies outperform their counterparts in stock price by a factor of 12. That's pretty cool, but here's where you'll really want to pay attention. In the absence of purpose, a company's leadership is likely to have greater difficulty in motivating employees and putting the company on the course to success. Customers are also likely to have difficulty connecting with the company. Bottom-line—Purpose isn't just good for those who consider being leaders (corporate/professional, community or even personal). Each of us needs to fully grasp that both as an individual and within our companies, no matter how large or small, Purpose adds significant positive value to those we serve, internally and externally; value that is far greater than the goods and/or services we provide.

When an organization's corporate purpose is congruent in the way it builds and upholds its culture and in how its strategic actions align, it can and will build, sustain, and increase trust, momentum, and loyalty. On the other hand, a corporate purpose that is incongruent with its culture and actions is like paint over rust; very quickly, it will be perceived with mistrust and skepticism.
By designing an authentic corporate purpose, one that is in alignment with the firm's strategic decisions and actions, a company will retain top talent, attract more clients, and will be perceived as a trustworthy company that walks the talk.

Magnetic North vs. True North

Here is a useful analogy: Three ships set sail from the same harbor to the same destination. The first ship has no compass but does have the expertise of an experienced crew. The second ship is equipped with a "Magnetic North" compass. The third ship is equipped with a compass that is set to "True North."

Despite its experienced, maybe even enthusiastic crew, the likelihood of the first ship reaching the correct destination is minuscule. The second ship will come closer to reaching the correct destination but could miss the mark by as much as 23 degrees as the magnetic pole slowly changes position along a predicted path.

Only a ship with a compass holding True North will accurately guide the captain to steer the ship, the crew, and all passengers to the desired destination. The impact of an authentic Purpose is like having a compass with a constant True North.
You may be thinking, "Okay Dov, I get it, that without Purpose, we may gather fabulous, enthusiastic people to us. However, keeping them will be, at best, very difficult, as the work will lack meaning. But what about your analogy of Magnetic North over True North?

On occasion, I am called in to an organization because they are having challenges with loyalty and or engagement. My team and I always begin by finding out if both the organization and the leader(s) inside the organization have clarified their Purpose. Sometimes they will tell us, "Yes, we hire XYZ consultants, and we developed our purpose."

You might be thinking the same thing I was the first time I heard this: Maybe it's not about Purpose. But you know what? Every time it was. You see, sometimes an individual or a company will have what we call a "Magnetic North" Purpose. What this means is that their purpose is generally pointed in the right direction. However, it's not "True North" because either the leader(s) purpose doesn't align with the company Purpose. Or the "purpose" is not a "True North" Purpose. Most likely, this happened because the purpose wasn't elicited using strategies that would allow the core team to be emotionally, as well as intellectually involved. Therefore, the magnetic North Purpose cannot be trusted, as the individual/company will get pulled to the next magnetic distraction. As a result, the talk becomes incongruent with the walk.

In the next chapter, we are going to veer a little away from looking at Purpose as a corporate thing and make it a little more personal.

CHAPTER TWO:

"I'LL BE HAPPY WHEN…"

Does more money and or more success makes us happier? Based on your personal bias it's easy to argue that it will, or won't. The truth is it could go either way depending on whether it's the end result or it's something that happens on the way to your end result.

Let me explain: In my career, I've met many successful leaders (you probably have too) who had all the trappings of success but who were deeply dissatisfied. Even with the beachfront homes, private planes, and enough discretionary income to finance a small country. Many of these individuals have worked around feeling (often secretly) that something was missing. To put it bluntly, below the surface all too often, the folks I'm referring to were basically very unhappy individuals who no matter how many more companies, pieces of property or toys they bought, they weren't getting any happier.

Bordering on Bitter

By the time they come to me, it's not unusual that they are often bordering on bitter.

You see, the challenge is that there's a very good chance that (like you) such a person is a peak performance individual. Maybe even the kind of person whom others look at and wonder how they could emulate because they consistently succeed at whatever they put themselves into.

While others struggle with confidence, no one would ever say that about these peak performance individuals. Anyone who knows them knows that they get things done. Having said that, there's also, a good chance that despite all the accolades, they can still feel like something significant, something vital, something that they just can't put their finger on is missing.

And as a result, they may even feel a little (or a lot) frustrated with themselves. You see because they (and maybe you see this in yourself) know that you're smart, so why can't they work it out? "If everything in the world doesn't make me happy, what's the point?" is often their unspoken question.

The answer, and it's not one they often want to hear, in that living a life that has been driven by "I'll Be Happy When..." (Fill in the ever-changing blank of objects, prestige, money, and even minions) may create temporary happiness, but in and of themselves, will never create any kind of lasting fulfillment.

Soul-seated Sense of Worth

The only thing that gives a person a deep, soul-seated sense of worth is living a meaningful, Purpose-driven life. Finding your Purpose is not another goal to be set on January 1st as a New Year's resolution. Discovering and living your Purpose moves you from success to significance, and on not just to happiness but to fulfillment. This is essential because without finding our Purpose we will continue to play the "I'll be happy when" game, which will inevitably continue to leave us with the insatiable hunger for more of something we can't pin down because we're not getting what it is that we truly desire.

When you don't know what it is that your heart and soul yearns for, all the efforts in the world won't give you the result you are seeking.

CHAPTER THREE:

REDEFINING LEADERS

I know that you might want to jump right into a process to get you genuinely connected to your Purpose, and I promise we will. However, before we do that, I want you and I to get totally on the same page…Is that okay with you?

If you are still reading, I'm going to take that as a yes!

Okay, let's take a moment and examine something vital to the context of having a "True North" Purpose. Because once we've done so, applying Purpose into how you live will not only make more sense, it will give you the fire your engine needs to live that Purpose.

Defining Leadership

For this reason, we need to agree on a definition for a leader. For me, a leader is not in and of itself a title or position. Many with such title and positions fail miserably to truly lead. What does that mean to you?

Leadership belongs to someone who has chosen to take up the mantle of impact and influence in moving towards their True Purpose. With that mantle comes the responsibility to guide, teach, and connect with an individual or a group of individuals in order to point them in a direction that aligns their hearts, minds, souls, and skills toward accomplishing a mutually desired goal or outcome… for the good of all concerned.

Let's take a moment to unpack that.

A leader has the ability to guide, teach, and connect. Put more simply, a leader is a person who can help others become their best selves (begin to see their "Deep Greatness") through the skillful use of direction, education (Latin definition: to draw out), and personal relationship.

Finding the Right Path

One important point: a leader can't lead everyone at all times. A leader has to know who she or he is leading in order to know what he or she is leading them towards. While some leadership skills cross disciplines, individuals don't. A doctor isn't simultaneously a CPA and a truck driver (at least not one I've ever met). A leader must be able to point toward the right path to accomplish a desired goal. Yes, there is a right path. There may not be a single path, but there is always a right path or at least a path that is right for the people involved. And that desired goal is a Definite Chief Aim. So, before you consider your Purpose, you need to think about yourself in terms of the previous definition. You may want to ask yourself the following questions:

1. Do I have the ability to guide, teach and connect? If not, do I want to learn these skills? (If you don't want to learn them, then there's no point in trying to become a leader.) If you do have that desire, you may want to consider where to go to improve these skills

2. Whom am I leading? Remember just because you are herding people in a general direction doesn't mean you are leading them. A sheepdog gets the sheep to the pen, but it's the shepherd who is doing the actual leading. You need to clearly understand whom you are leading—other leaders? Managers? Workers? Peers? Subordinates? A community?

3. What paths are out there? Which one is the right path for my endeavor? This may take some soul-searching because it can be hard to see other paths when you are deeply committed to one direction. However, stepping back and looking for alternatives is essential in order to come to the final question.

4. What is my desired goal? Now, it's easy to say the desired goal is greater profit or more growth or whatever other economic metric you want to use, but when you define your goal purely in terms of economics, lasting satisfaction and happiness will continually elude you. Hence the pursuit of Purpose.

Defining DCA

Now that we have some basis of agreement on leadership, we can talk about DCA. A Definite Chief Aim is something that gives you and what you are doing "meaning" because it is aligned with "Purpose." It's the reason you get up in the morning. It's the reason you do what you do each day.

Too many leaders think their Purpose is to make money for themselves (their families) or even the corporation. While that can be a reason, it's not a Purpose. Steve Jobs certainly wanted to make money. It was one of the reasons that he founded Apple. But his Purpose was more than profit. He had an idea, a vision, of how electronics could transform the world. As he said, "Being the richest man in the cemetery doesn't matter to me. Going to bed at night saying we've done something wonderful... that's what matters to me." That's Purpose!

Having a DCA that is aligned with your Purpose is what allows you to go to bed at night believing that you have done something wonderful. A word of caution: Don't fall into the trap of thinking that "something wonderful" has to be mind-blowing and huge. A parent who has helped a child take a few first tentative steps has done "something wonderful" that day if the parent's DCA is ultimately to raise an independent adult. As a leader, if your Purpose is to help create a motivated, creative, and passionate team, then the excitement you see on the face of someone who is solving a problem can very well be your "something wonderful."

Finally, it's time to talk about how to determine YOUR Purpose.

CHAPTER FOUR:

PASSION AND PURPOSE

By now you are probably thinking, "Okay, so I need to discover my Purpose, but how do I figure it out?" Don't worry—this is where a lot of people get stuck. Often a person might think that their Purpose is somehow going to drop out the sky and clobber them on the head. It doesn't work that way (except in extreme cases like my own. See "About the Author" and it will become crystal clear). Or, they look at it as something overwhelming, and they throw in the towel before they even get in the game.

Take comfort in knowing that finding your Purpose is a process; one that you have to undertake with a certain amount of courage and determination, but you will get there. The bad news is that no one can do it for you. The good news is that there is a process that will get you there and once you have determined your own true Purpose no one can take it from you.

Let's begin by thinking of people you know or have heard of who have lived their Purpose. You might consider people like Steve Jobs, Martin Luther King, Gandhi, or Mother Teresa. Or perhaps it is someone you know personally such as a mentor or a friend.

Now consider what they have in common. Yes, people as outwardly different as Steve Jobs and Mother Teresa do share at least one trait: they were all Purpose-driven.

Purpose Vs. Passion

As far back as the 1990s, the idea of following your passion was very in vogue. As wonderful as that was at getting people out of jobs they hated, many folks found themselves financially destitute and feeling like they did something wrong because their "passion" didn't lead to profit. Don't get me wrong. I'm a big fan of passion. I'm a passionate guy. But passion without Purpose will end up leaving you struggling for something far more meaningful.

So, what do I mean by "Purpose-driven"? Let's approach it this way. All too often we think that Purpose is found in passion. I know you might find it shocking, but it isn't! Your Purpose and your passion are not the same thing. They may be related, but they aren't the same and never will be.

Your passion is transitory. In other words, your passion may and probably will change over time. When you are in your 20s, you may be passionate about snowboarding, but in your 70s you may be passionate about stamp collecting. (Or vice versus.) Passion often depends on many external factors—your age, your health, your finances, where you live, who you associate with. These things are all changeable, and as they change, so, too, will your passion.

Your Purpose, on the other hand, is the undercurrent that flows throughout your life. It is with you during your snowboarding days and it remains in your stamp collecting moments. How you live your passion may, and probably will change, but your Purpose is an essential part of your core being. That's why it's so important to find your Purpose because when you do, I assure you that your passion will find you!

Let's look at two of the people in the list above. You might be tempted to say that Martin Luther King's Purpose was ministry or Mother Teresa's passion was serving the poor. But let me challenge you to see a bigger picture; to see that those were their passions and not their Purposes.

Martin Luther King's Purpose was to eliminate racial discrimination. The way he did that was through his passion for preaching and ministry. He could have had that very same Purpose but lived it out with a different passion—perhaps government service. And, conversely, he could have had a passion for ministry that grew out of a very different Purpose. Consider televangelists whose passion for preaching grows out of a Purpose to get rich!

Or look at Mother Teresa. Her Purpose was to demonstrate that all people have worth and value. She did that by her passion for serving the poor. Need proof? She was in her 40s before she began working with the poor. Before that, she lived out her Purpose by teaching in a girls' school. Same Purpose. Different expressions. Different passions.

CHAPTER 5:

WHERE PURPOSE HIDES AND HOW TO FIND IT

How are you enjoying this book so far? Getting some genuine insights? Are you starting to think about things at a deeper level? Wonderful!

That being said you may not like what I'm going to say next. You find your passion in your pleasure, but you find your Purpose in your pain. Your true Purpose is always hidden underneath your pain. If you want to find your Purpose, you must look at your pain. (Don't worry we're not talking about ten years of sitting in a therapists office) We're on the fast track here, so let's jump in…)

Finding The One Red Thread… Step 1

Ask yourself the following questions (and answer them):

Part 1. What bothers you? What really bothers you in the world?

Part 2. What has bothered you as long as you can remember?

Part 3. What would you remove from the planet if time and money were no obstacle?

A note of caution: The temptation is to keep answers on the surface and not dig deep enough to find the Purpose that will be there. Do NOT give in to easy. For instance, let's say you have always been bothered by untidiness. You can't stand a mess; anything that is out of place creates real irritation, even pain for you. You could think that your Purpose in life is to eliminate all messes. Or it might be to ensure that nothing in your home is ever out of place, but I'd argue that not only isn't possible, it's not your Purpose. (It might be your passion, but remember Purpose and passion aren't the same.)

Only you can answer for sure, but I'd offer that your Purpose might be to make it easier for people to keep things tidy. To that end, you might focus on a different kind of home organizational system or a new recycling model. Maybe it's a new way to dispose of trash. Or a way to motivate people to see how to keep the planet clean. Or…well, you get the idea. Your pain at messes may actually be tied to your Purpose being around creating a better world. Starting to get the feel of it?

Push and Pull

Some people are twenty pounds overweight and they get up in the morning and go to the gym on a rainy day because they hate the way their body looks. Other people get up on that same rainy morning with their own twenty pounds of excess weight and go to the gym because they are looking forward to feeling sexy in that outfit they've had their eye on. The first person is primarily motivated by pain; the second is motivated primarily by pleasure. (Although each of us has our own primary motivator (pleasure or pain), no one is motivated exclusively by one or the other)

No matter who we are, where we're from or what we do, it's important to realize that Pleasure and Pain are, to some degree, the primary motivating factors of "all" human beings.

Here's the power of it: Pleasure tends to move us in the short term and is what we prefer. Pain moves us long terms. We only achieve fulfillment by accessing the Purpose that is hidden under the pain.

CHAPTER 6:

FULL MONTY PURPOSE ELICITATION® PROCESS

All right, are you ready to roll up your sleeves and dive right into the process of finding your Purpose?

We are about to do an exercise. Before we begin, let me offer you both a few words of caution and share an example of encouragement. The caution: If you wimp out you won't get what you came here for! Be courageous! You are worth it because the rewards of being on Purpose are life-changing. Let me share this example of encouragement:

> When Franco walked into my office, I was instantly taken by his big, warm, inviting smile. He was already very successful and considered by many to be a top consultant in his field. He seemed to have it all—brand new convertible Mercedes, a house overlooking the ocean, not to mention he was working high net worth individuals and families. Plus he had a wine cellar that wine enthusiasts would have paid money to visit.
>
> But secretly there was sadness about him. He described it as a constant sense of impending doom. Like more than 70 percent of high performers, he had a sincere sense that he was going to at any moment be discovered as a fraud.

All of Franco's external success had done a good job of hiding these feelings from the world, but he could no longer hide them from himself.

As we began working together, I saw in him something magnificent. I saw in him access to his true Purpose, and with it potential that he had never touched in all of his success. It was something so great that when I first spoke to him about it, he told me he had no idea what I was talking about.

Through our work, I earned his trust enough to challenge him to look at how he might be perpetuating the very things that were causing him pain. When I asked him to look at how what was happening might have its root in his ,history, he told me, "I've looked at that stuff, it's all in the past, I've just got to move on," but clearly his past was leaking all over his present.

On one occasion he landed a big contract and then sabotaged it by emotionally vomiting on the prospective client. In his personal life, he would walk in a room and find himself dynamically attracted to the woman he described as having "angry eyes." Needless to say, those relationships always became a source of pain.

Explaining that his Purpose was hidden beneath his pain, I asked him if he had the courage to look at what he truly needed. (Not surface things like more money, or another sexual encounter, but rather the need that was driving his behavior). He said he was courageous enough, and within a short period of time, he stopped showing up for appointments. He ran away. I knew clearly we were close to the bone.

Some time passed and when he finally came back, he admitted that he had run away and told me he was back because something I had said kept echoing in his mind: "Who will suffer if you continue to play small, and ignore your Purpose?"

You see even though he was playing big by other people's standards, he was playing small compared to what he intuitively knew that he came to the planet to do.

This time we turned to what Joseph Campbell called his "dark cave," the place he had feared to look, to discover the thing he had always needed. Not because his parents were bad, but simply because it was what he needed. What we discovered was that the bullying behavior he would sometime display, his incessant need for money and sexual conquests had a common theme — *The One Red Thread*.

Our (unconscious) One Red Thread is usually double-edged. While it remains unconscious, it will likely drive us to repeat what didn't work. We hope and believe we can make it different this time, while often repeating the same old behaviors.

You did Step 1 in chapter 5 so now on to:

Step 2: Finding *The One Red Thread* that will give you access to your Purpose begins by imagining your own funeral.

Imagine that you are invisibly floating around, looking at everyone and hearing everything. I don't know if you've ever been to a funeral, but if you have, you'll know exactly what I'm talking about. The job of the person giving the eulogy is to dry clean the life of the person who died. In other words, he or she is saying all the nice and right things one says at a funeral.

Okay, come back to imaging that you are invisibly floating around as the person at the front is delivering your eulogy. You are listening to the very best version of who you were.

Let me ask you: **What is that person delivering the eulogy saying about you? (Remember; it's only the very best stuff)** Write down what you would really want them to say: Warning do NOT skip this (or any part of this exercise. Remember you bought this book so that you could find your Purpose)

Having written down your answer now answer, How does it make you feel to be described in such terms?

Step 3: You are still at the service, still invisible to everyone, now floating to the back.

> Find yourself hovering over those back pews where the people who either didn't really know you or like you might be sitting. As you linger there, listen to what the people who aren't dry cleaning who you were are saying.
>
> What do you hear? Moreover, what do you fear you will hear?
>
> These things don't have be some huge secret offense, just what might be said about you in the deepest whispers. What painful truths are they revealing?
>
> Write it down! Now write down how you feel being described in such terms?

Most often what is said at the back is a direct contradiction of what's being said at the front. If what they are saying at the front doesn't make you tingle with excitement, keep going. You're not there yet!

If what they are whispering in the back doesn't make you either sincerely sad or mad. You're not there yet. Dig deeper!

Step 4: The Push-Pull That Reveals your True Purpose

I'm going to walk you through the process that will pull it all together, but first let me give you look into someone else's world so that you can see how it plays out.

To help you pull it all together, let's go back to Franco's answers as an example:

Step 1: What had always bothered him was "feeling like an outsider." What he would have wanted to remove from the planet was "bullying."

Step 2: His Idealized Eulogy: "He was a deeply loving and giving man, who personally and professionally brought families together."

Step 3: The Whispers in the Pews. (What he didn't want to hear but feared might be said). "He was needy man who, when he didn't get what he wanted, would bully until he got what he wanted and then he would dismiss those who gave in to his coercion."

As you read through his answers, you can likely see his *One Red Thread*. Remember until it's revealed, our One Red Thread usually plays out in a less than healthy manner. However, when it's revealed, there are wonderful opportunities for that very same One Read Thread to transform who we are and how we operate in the world, as well as to see the massive impact we can have.

Got a sense of it now? Don't worry about trying to get it right, it's okay to go through the exercise and come back to it may times until it really hits.

Now it's your turn:

Take out a pen and paper: (Yes, I know it's old school, but the research shows that when dealing with things that have emotional roots, writing by hand always works better.)

Flip back and look at what you wrote earlier for your answer in **Step 1** regarding what bothers you (has always bothered you), and what you would remove from the planet if time and money were no obstacle.

Now write out your answers to the pull of your idealized self (front of the room eulogy).

Step 2. Directly below the eulogy write down the push away from the whispers in the pews in **Step 3**.

Step 4: If you have genuinely dug deep, you will be able to begin to see that One Red Thread that runs through all three answers. Often it's something that looks negative in how it shows up in your world, but it is, in fact, calling you to heal it within yourself and in turn, within your world.

By the way, here's what happened with Franco when he found his "One Red Thread":

> When we boiled it down, Franco was able to see that the hunger for power that had shown up in the need to control others, create sexual conquests, build status, and earn money was tied to this One Red Thread by nothing more than the part of him that had always needed an emotionally "Safe Space."
>
> However, until the thread was revealed, it continued to be tied to doing things in a way that proved not only to be destructive but even make it unsafe for himself and others. In other words, he was creating the very thing he didn't want by repeating what was familiar to him.
>
> When he began to fully realize that his One Red Thread was that what he had always needed and couldn't get or couldn't get enough of was "safe space," he accessed his "Purpose" and set about discovering how he could actually assist those he served in his business by creating a *Safe Space* for themselves and their loved ones.
>
> The result is that not only is Franco the bestselling author of the book "Safe Space," he let go of his prestigious ocean view property and now lives downtown in a place that he describes as his physical "Safe Space." His relationships have transformed into deeply loving and supportive ones, and on top of that, he now works internationally with clients he loves who love him. He is regarded by many as the #1 player in his niche, and as a result, is bringing in record profits.

Congratulations. You've found the path to your Purpose.

CHAPTER 7:

WHAT'S NEXT?

Now that you have, at the very least, found the opening to your Purpose or at least are on the way to figuring out, it's only natural to ask what's next?

As leaders in our own lives, and the lives of others, we need to think about the difference between purpose and goals. As a leader, you've been taught to think in terms of goals—daily, monthly, annual, financial, personal. You may even have a spreadsheet of all your goals.

Goals, Purpose, and Direction

Now goals are important, but they aren't the same thing as your Purpose. Goals can be markers that help you determine where you are on the path to your Purpose. Before you start to think that I'm downgrading goals, I'm not. I believe that it's valuable to set goals, but you must be clear that moving towards a goal and moving towards your Purpose, could be, but is not necessarily the same thing.

Let's say you want to take a road trip from New York to California. You plug LA into your GPS and set out on the highway. Now the GPS is going to tell you the fastest route to LA-LA Land. It's probably going to take you through some pretty desolate country in the middle of the United States, but it's always going to point you toward LA. Every day you can set a goal of how many miles you need to drive and set about achieving that goal.

Along the way, you might see a sign advertising Tony's Tremendous Truckstop. If you take the turn, you will end up heading the opposite direction from LA. You will not meet your mileage goal for the day. But…and this is important, there's nothing wrong with deciding you want to take the detour. It's your life, after all.

So you turn off and check out the burgers and fries at Tony's Tremendous Truckstop. When you are done, you get back in the car. At this point; without the GPS you may get hopelessly off course and keep heading north to the Canadian border, but your GPS will recalculate and give you a new route to LA. If indeed you find yourself off course, you may need to set a new mileage goal, because your route has changed. You may not reach LA at the exact time you planned, but because you have your GPS set, you can reset a goal and continue on your cross-country trip.

The same is true with your Purpose. You can set short-term goals to show you if you are moving closer or further away from your ultimate Purpose. These goals help you evaluate where you are, but they are markers on the journey to your Purpose, not the Purpose itself.

Being a Purpose-driven leader is an honor and a responsibility because you will be serving those who are in alignment with your Purpose. Treat this responsibility with respect. Part of that respect is in knowing that there will always be those who feel (some with very good reasons) that your Purpose does not align with theirs.
Being on Purpose does not give you the right to make those who have not found their Purpose, or who feel their Purpose is not aligned with yours, they are wrong or a failure. We each have our path and our own timing.

Closing thoughts:

As we move towards the end of this book, I would like to share one of the fundamental precepts of both the private leadership work that I do for founders, entrepreneurs, C-Suite leaders, CEOs, entertainers, athletes, and organizations. I share it with you here so that you might realize the full power and impact of your fully stepping into, claiming, and refining your Purpose and then sharing it with those you lead.

My belief (not necessarily THE truth) **is that the reason we go into leadership** (in and form) **is to reconcile our soul.** Before you run off thinking I'm on some woo-woo rant, give me a moment.

What I mean by "we go into leadership is to reconcile our soul" is that we seek to bring home the disenfranchised parts of ourselves that we have had to compartmentalize for social and familial reasons. (The parts of us that were rejected by others or even ourselves.) We lead because it is in leading that we ourselves are given the opportunity to remember the complete person we are meant to be.

The other side of this is that we lead so that we can serve. By that I mean that when we are genuine Purpose-driven leaders, we serve others by helping them return to wholeness through the venue of what we do for leadership.

Our leadership helps shine light into the blind spots of those we lead, but a genuine leader who has successfully determined his or her True Purpose also shines light into their own blind spots. Nothing brings a leader down faster than ignoring a blind spot and nothing shed light on a blind spot faster than a well-thought-out-felt-into Purpose.

1 - https://hbr.org/resources/pdfs/comm/ey/19392HBRReportEY.pdf

GRATITUDES

My sincere gratitude to everyone who has in their own way added to this book. First off my gratitude to the man who started out a client, became a student, and has evolved into a courageous friend —Francesco Lombardo. Thank you for permission to use your *"One Red Thread"* story. You are a shining example of what happens when we have the courage to look at what we are doing and is it really honoring the legacy we want to leave and as a result creating "Safe Space".

My gratitude to my wonderful, patient editor Woodeene Koenig-Bricker. Your ability to bring together my ramblings into something that even resembles good English while keeping it "Dov" is a genuine blessing to me, and the work I do.

My gratitude to my "Advisory board" for helping me pull in the multitude of ideas and help me see what is wanted and needed that I have the honor of providing.

Finally, thank you to you dear reader. Thank you for buying this book, spreading the word about the work we (my company and I) do. But most of all thank you for having the courage to find your *One Red Thread* Because by you living and leading from your own true Purpose, you help those you interact with remember that they too are worthy of claiming their whole self.

No one does it alone! I'd like to thank my friends and board of advisers, each of you, individually and collectively inspires me.

Thank you for being a beacon of light shining my life and the lives that you impact.

We all have our blind spots, thank you for loving me enough to see mine, and share with me how I can better fulfil my own purpose in order to have the impact I came in here to have.

Renuka Baron - Certified Communication Expert. Licensed NLP Practitioner. Full-partner, co-facilitator and mentor at Dov Baron International and Authentic Paragon Alliance.

Mark Levy - Positioning and Branding Consultant and Founder of Levy Innovation LLC. Writer for the New York Times. Writer/Co-Creater of five books including the acclaimed "Accidental Genius: Using Writing to Generate Your Best Ideas, Insight, and Content."

Tony Grebmeier - Founder of multi-million dollar business INC 5000 business, Ship Offers. Host of BE FULFILLED podcast.

Joel Bower - CEO of Skirmish Strategies. Business Consultant to help drive momentum & leverage for growth.

Jim Bouchard - Corporate & Conference Speaker and Executive Mentor at Black Belt Mindset Productions LLC. Founder and Managing Editor at San Chi Publishing. Candidate for United States Congress

Joshua Miller - Master Certified Executive & Personal Coach. TEDx Speaker. Author of "I CALL BULLSHIT: Live Your Life, Not Someone Else's

Jared Nichols - Futurist, advisor, and faculty member at the University of Tennessee Haslam College of Business, in Graduate and Executive Education. Host of the Podcast, "The Road Ahead: Small Business in the 21st Century,"

Damian Loth - Publisher at Men's Essentials Magazine. Partner at Media in Motion LLC. Official Sponsor of the Jamaican Bobsled Team.

Recently I celebrated my 60th birthday... Wow!

My bride held an open house for our friends to drop by at 3PM and they stayed all the way until 2:30 AM. By the end of the day our place looked like a Mexican florist's. Everyone who knows me knows I love flowers and tequila and there was no shortage of either.

My bride had created a 12 hour playlist of my favorite music, we danced, we talked we laughed and then at around 8PM, some people decided to share what started out as their personal birthday wishes.

However, it quickly turned into something that would have me rethink the work I do, how and most importantly; why I do it.

Almost every single one of my close friends spoke about how when we'd met they had felt resistant to meeting me. They all spoke about how they felt; I could/would see through whatever façade they had (some said they didn't even know they had one until that very moment).

What I didn't expect was that each of them said something in the realm of:

"Without you I'd never have been able to (fill in the blank)."

"What you saw in me, and brought out (Some might say say **dragged out**) has shifted me to live my life on purpose, and the impact I'm having in the world has made my life and the lives I touch more fulfilling."

I stood there for an hour, shaking, with tears rolling down my cheeks, completely awash in gratitude.

You see, here I was; thinking I was a leadership expert (and I am), while ironically, at the core of what I do (that I couldn't see) was help people see what they cannot see in themselves; their genius, their brilliance, and their purpose.

In one of my books entitled: "Don't Read This Unless You Want More Money" I called this; Your Genius Blind-spot. **I teach this stuff** and there I was smack in the middle of my own Genius Blind-spot. It goes to show how crucial it is to have someone you trust help you see what you can't.

I want to ask you a quick question. Have you ever asked yourself…

- What exactly is *my* purpose?

- What is that value that I have given or could give to all those around me?

- What is that thing everyone else sees in me that I can't?

- What is my own Genius Blind-spot and what has it cost me?

If you have been asking any of these, I would love to give you the opportunity to have me walk you through this process ***personally*** to answer each and every one of those questions and turn them from your Blind-Spot to biggest strength.

If this sounds like something that you've been desiring and has held you back, head here to get all of the details > *https://purpose.fullmontyleadership.com/sign-up-find-your-purpose-waitlist.*

Sincerely,

Dov

ABOUT THE AUTHOR

Dov Baron: Twice cited as one of Inc. Magazine's Top 100 Leadership Speakers to hire, also cited in the Meeting and Event Professionals Guide to The Top 100 Motivational Speakers and Named as one of the Top 30 Global Leadership Guru's.

Dov is a man with a finger on the pulse of the evolving world of NextGen leadership.

He is a bestselling author of several books. His latest book is Fiercely Loyal; How High Performing Companies Develop and Retain Top Talent. He is the host of the national (US) TV show "Pursuing Deep Greatness with Dov Baron" on ROKU TV, and the host of the Number One Podcast for Fortune 500 Listeners (globally) "Dov Baron's Leadership and Loyalty Show" on iTunes and is carried on FM & AM Radio Stations across the US.

He also writes for and has been featured in many industry magazines including being featured on CNN, CBS Small Business Pulse, SHRM, Yahoo Finance, Boston Globe, Business in

Vancouver, USA today, CEO, Entrepreneur and many more.

Dov Baron has been speaking internationally for over 30 years. Dov Baron has had the honor of presenting for many esteemed audiences including; US Air Force, The Servant Leadership Institute, The World Business Conference in Tehran The State Department, and The United Nations. He is considered by many as a leading authority on Authentic Leadership. Dov is also the founder of Full Monty Leadership and The Authentic Speaker Academy for Leadership.

Outside of his speaking and training, Dov works privately with multi-disciplinary leaders and executive teams to build the bonds that create organizational cultures that become Fiercely Loyal.

Life-Changing Story:

In June 1990, while free rock climbing, Dov Baron fell approximately 120 feet and landed on his face. The impact shattered most of the bone structure of his face, disintegrating some of his upper jaw and fracturing his lower jaw in four places. After nine reconstructive surgeries, no external evidence remains of the damage; however, this experience was life-changing.

Before the fall, Dov had spent years building a reputation as a dynamic speaker and teacher in the field of personal and professional development, but it wasn't until years after the fall that he began to see the beauty and elegance of what had really happened – the return to his own CORE –what he calls his 'Authentic Self'.

Today

Today, Dov has been sharing his wisdom and expertise privately and on international stages with professional leaders for more than 30 years. Dov's influence has created a massive social media platform with over 200,000 followers via Facebook, Twitter, LinkedIn, Podomatic, iTunes, etc.

He has interviewed and worked with leaders featured on Oprah, Ellen, CNN, Fox, MSNBC, CBS, Huffington Post, Larry King, New York Times, Washington Post, Forbes, the Wall Street Journal and many other top-rated media.

Dov's "KIllTheKeynote" campaign to change the speaking industry went viral to over 5 million people on social media. He is now speaking for some of Europe's wealthiest families at Scone Palace, Next-Gen leaders with UnleashWD and the Legacy Show, and top American c-suite leaders for The #CSuite Network.

In addition to being an author and a radio host, Dov is also the leading expert on Developing Authentic Leadership and he is the world's only Corporate Cultural Momentum Strategist, serving top performance individuals, corporations and organizations to generate both exponential growth and fierce loyalty.

His passion mixed with humor and 'get to the point' no BS style are contagious. Within moments, you will feel a genuine connection with a man who authentically walks his talk. Dov believes that the world needs more leaders who are Authentically committed to living their Purpose, standing in their truth, sharing their inner genius, and empowering others to do the same.

Dov's commitment is to take you by the hand and show you why tapping into your Authentic Self is the MOST important key to finding, developing, and retaining your top talent.

To engage Dov Baron for media interviews, one-on-one as an Impact Strategist, speaking at your events, or consulting at your organization, please write to…

Admin@DovBaron.com
or call +1-778-379-7517.

FullMontyLeadership.com

FullMontyLeadership.com

@TheDovBaron

Printed in Great Britain
by Amazon